Books by Beverly Russell from Amazon.com

Designers' Workplaces

Architecture and Design 1970-1990

Women of Design

Forty Under Forty

Women of Taste

Six

Design Does Matter

The Adventures of Kundun the Golden Cat
(with Benjamin Beardwood)

Crossings

Espacios – Jardines de San Miguel

Garden Tarot Card Pack

Ask the Flowers
(with Gillian Redfern Rones)

Lines on Aging

Beverly Russell

Photography
by Barry Michlin

Lines on Aging

Beverly Russell

Copyright 2013

Beverly Russell

ISBN 978-0-9762905-3-7

Published by Beverly Russell Enterprises

High Falls, NY 12440

www.beverlyrussell.com

Graphic design and layout by Julissa Diaz

Photography by Barry Michlin

Printing by Lightning Source International

Library of Congress cataloging in progress

For Benjamin, the Good Shepherd

Contents

Preface by Dh. Kiranada 11

Introduction by Beverly Russell 15

Poetry and prose.. 16-65

Credits 67-9

List of photographs 71

Index to quotations 72-77

Preface
Dh. Kiranada

I look at aging as a Spiritual Practice, with the knowledge that everything is going to vanish, including me. The poets know this; the sages speak of it often and yet western society encourages us to ignore it. As a young person who was raised with wise elders, I watched aging carefully -- and took notes. I saw those who denied it and hid from it; those who railed against it and sadly, those who later lived their lives full of regret.

Aging can be uncomfortable when it puts us in touch with our own impermanence. To depart, with gratitude and grace has been my wish for many years; to depart with gratitude for all I have been given; for my connections with beings around the world; for all those who have been generous in their kindness to others and the teachings and care they have given me. With gratitude and grace I hope to drop that ego, to generate equanimity, to share loving kindness -- and to dwell between the breaths.

The indignities of old age are real. Impermanence is real. When I was a teenager, I had a sharp awakening, with my father's sudden death. At that time, I made a personal promise to not live a life of regret but to be present to the moment; to live fully and intentionally; to travel and embrace the world's people; to express beauty and love – in my case, through art. Some of the wonder of that aspiration is caught by the poet Mary Oliver:
"When it is all over, I want to say: All my life
I was a bride married to amazement,
I was a bridegroom, taking the world into my arms".

I want to be present for each moment because, I am aware that we really do not know about the next moment – or the next year. My long practice of meditation is core to my own mindfulness training.

The mystic poet Rabindranath Tagore, here in this wonderful book, also counsels me: to be fearless when facing dangers, to have the heart to conquer pain, to find friends along the road, and to have the patience to win freedom. The freedom that I seek is the freedom, the liberation, the awakening that Buddha spoke of under the Bodhi tree, 2500 years ago.

And so – here is a road and a wise path for life that may come to fruition in our later years. In my thirst for that wisdom (and with the support of many friends) I have set aside my seventieth year to slip out of this world and go on a retreat – for twelve months; to sit in silence, alone, 10,000 miles from home; opening myself to this spiritual practice, for all beings.

May you live each day – and may you be well.

Introduction

Beverly Russell

"Age is an issue of mind over matter. If you don't mind, it doesn't matter," wrote Mark Twain. Nevertheless, there comes a time when denial is unrealistic. At this point, it is useful to examine the Buddhist sequence of events that describes a pattern of aging: "Lightning Strikes," "Getting Control," "Adaptation," and "Appreciation." "Lightning" has already struck me (physical parts have worn out). "Getting control" of this situation has led me to make the "adaptation" necessary as an octogenarian. From here on I look with "appreciation" at my life scenario.

The poetry and commentaries gathered into this collection have given me strength to carry on and be glad while enjoying the fruits of the final years and the reality of closure, and to look forward to checking into a world of angels. Barry Michlin's accompanying mystical photographs lift the spirits and hint at the promise of enlightenment to come.

Reality Check

Aging is a biological process when your body goes to hell on you and falls apart. Aging is the time of life when you become more fragile. If you're 80 and ice skating with a young friend of 30 and you both take a fall, you are most likely to be the one who ends up with a broken bone.

There is no free lunch. There is even a technical term for aging "negative pleiotropy" the notion that a genetic trait gives you advantages earlier in life at the cost of disadvantages later on.

Aging is a time of life when organisms don't deal with stress very well. Lots of stress throughout the lifetime will accelerate the aging process and there is endless scientific evidence for this.

Dr. Robert Sapolsky, Stress and Aging

Stages

As every flower fades and as all youth
Departs, so life at every stage,
So every virtue, so our grasp of truth,
Blooms in its day and may not last forever.
Be ready, heart, for parting, new endeavor,
Be ready bravely and without remorse
To find new light that old ties cannot give.
In all beginnings dwells a magic force
For guarding us and helping us to life.

Serenely let us move to distant places
And let no sentiments of home detain us.
The Cosmic Spirit seeks not to restrain us
But lifts us stage by stage to wider spaces.
If we accept a home of our own making,
Familiar habit makes for indolence.
We must prepare for parting and leave-taking
Or else remain the slaves of permanence....

Hermann Hesse, Magister Ludi

Awareness

Aging people should know that their lives are not mounting and unfolding but that an inexorable inner process forces the contraction of life. For a young person it is almost a sin – and certainly a danger – to be too much occupied with self; but for the aging person it is a duty and a necessity to give serious attention to self.

Carl Gustav Jung, Modern Man in Search of a Soul

Appreciation

As a white candle
In a holy place
So is the beauty
Of an aged face

Joseph Campbell, The Old Woman

Cycles

Birth, and copulation, and death.
That's all the facts when you come to brass tacks.

T.S Eliot, Sweeney Agonistes

Accepting

"Well, I'm old," said Lady Matilda Cleckheaton. "Yes, I'm old. Of course, you don't know what it is to be old. If it isn't one thing it's another. Rheumatism or arthritis or a nasty bit of asthma or a sore throat or an ankle you've turned. Always something, you know. Nothing very important. But there it is. .."

"I've got a few old friends left, you know… Of course, most of them are either practically stone deaf or half blind or a little bit gone in the top storey or unable to walk straight. But something still functions. Something, shall we say, up here." She hit the top of her neatly arranged white head…."Unfortunately, old age doesn't get cured, it only gets more so, doesn't it?"

Agatha Christie, Passenger to Frankfurt

Reflection

Let me not pray to be sheltered
from dangers
But be fearless in facing them.
Let me not beg for the stilling of my pain
but for the heart to conquer it.
Let me not look for allies in life's battles
but to my own strength
Let me not crave in anxious fear
to be saved
But hope for the patience to win
my freedom

Rabindranath Tagore

Support

It is my family that helps me face the unavoidable problems of age and the inevitable loss of friends…

I've been fortunate in life-style, in health, and in having so many interests, but old age is no barrel of laughs. Even if you are generally healthy, there are things – your heart (atrial fibrillation), your hips (arthritis), general slowing down mentally and physically – that make denial of aging an impossibility. People begin to take your arm, ask if you want an elevator, and generally treat you like a relic. Though they have nothing but the best and most solicitous of motives, it's hard not to be condescended to.

It's dangerous when you are older to start living in the past. Now that it's out of my system, I intend to live in the present, looking forward to the future.

Katharine Graham, A Personal History

Listening

When I was a seminary student, my teacher demanded enthusiasm. He taught us four things that would feed it: wanting to be enthusiastic; sticking with it; letting ourselves be happy; and being careful not to get too carried away because that could lead to having-to-lie-on-the-floor exhaustion.

We had to choose enthusiasm, something that doesn't come naturally in a society that is already rushing us through our days. If we couldn't feel it immediately, we had to give it a little time to kick in. For most of us, especially those of us reared in the land of cynicism, this meant not judging ourselves, or him, too harshly too soon. Along the same line, we had to give ourselves permission to feel the joy that is a by-product of enthusiasm. Joy can be a little embarrassing if you aren't used to it. It feels a little too Hallmark TV channelish. A little false. Except it isn't. It's true and it feeds our happiness, our health and our sanity and it balances out the inevitable sorrows in our lives.

Geri Larkin, Plant Seed, Pull Weed

Rationalizing

Illness happens. It is not something exceptional, it is part of nature and a fact of life. Of course, we have every right to avoid illness and pain, but in spite of that effort, when illness happens it is better to accept it. While you should make every effort to cure it as soon as possible, you should have no extra mental burden. As the great Indian scholar Shantideva has said: "If there is a way to overcome the suffering, then there is no need to worry, if there is no way to overcome the suffering, then there is no use in worrying." That kind of rational attitude is quite useful.

The Dalai Lama's Book of Wisdom

Maturing

Oh, roses for the flush of youth,
And laurel for the perfect prime;
But pluck an ivy branch for me
Grown old before my time.

Christina Georgina Rosetti, Oh Roses for the Flush

Remembering

I sit beside the fire and think of all that I have seen
Of meadow flowers and butterflies
in summers that have been
Of yellow leaves and gossamer
in autumns that there were
With morning mist and silver sun
and wind upon my hair
I sit beside the fire and think
of how the world will be
When winter comes without a spring
that I shall ever see.
For still there are so many things
that I have never seen
In every wood in every spring
There is a different green.
I sit beside the fire and think
Of people long ago,
And people who will see a world
that I shall never know
But all the while I sit and think
of times there were before
I listen for returning feet and voices at the door

J.R.R. Tolkien, The Road Goes Ever On

Carpe Diem

Gather ye rosebuds while ye may,
Old Time is still a-flying;
And this same flower that smiles to-day,
Tomorrow will be dying.

The glorious lamp of Heaven, the sun,
The higher he's a getting;
The sooner will his race be run,
And nearer he's to setting.

Robert Herrick, To Virgins to Make Much of Time

Evolving

Our souls hunger for the lost connection to our intuitive nature expressed through myths, dreams, stories and images. We long for a creative, symbolic process that nurtures our spiritual nature, that feeds the soul.

We begin to nourish ourselves spiritually when we discover the dimensions of divine/human consciousness, when we begin to discover the Divine within. We need to understand that the spirit of creation lives and evolves within each human being, as well as through the whole of the created order. Many of us sense this mysterious unfolding. And many are seeking experiences that help us to respond to the changes this evolution brings into our lives.

Dr. Lauren Artress, Walking a Sacred Path

Wisdom

Without going out of doors
You can know the ways of the world

Without looking out the window
You can know the ways of heaven

The farther you go outward, the less you know

Thus, the sage knows without going outward
Understands without looking outward
Accomplishes without acting outward

Yasuhiko Genku Kimura, translated From Lao Tzu's The Book of Balance

Relinquishing

Then loudly cried the bold Sir Bedivere:
"Ah! My Lord Arthur, wither shall I go?
Where shall I hide my forehead and my eyes?
For now I see the true old times are dead,
When every morning brought a noble chance,
And every chance brought out a noble knight…
And slowly answer'd Arthur from the barge:
"The old order changeth, yielding place to new.…
So said he, and the barge with oar and sail
Moved from the brink, like some full-breasted swan
That, fluting a wild carol ere her death,
Ruffles her pure cold plume, and takes the flood
With swarthy webs. Long stood Sir Bedivere,
Revolving many memories, till the hull
Look'd one black dot against the verge of dawn…
The stillness of the dead world's winter dawn
Amazed him, and he groan'd, "The King is gone."
And therewithal came on him the weird rhyme,
"From the great deep to the great deep he goes…"
"He passes to be King among the dead."

Alfred Tennyson, Idylls of the King

Focussing

An elder said: A man who keeps death before his eyes will at all times overcome his cowardice.

Thomas Merton, The Wisdom of the Desert

.. Even the hour of our death may send
Us speeding on to fresh and newer spaces,
And life may summon us to newer races.
So be it, heart: bid farewell without end.

Herman Hesse, Stages, Magister Ludi

Believing

I often recalled asking Ravelstein which of his friends were likely to follow him. "To keep you company," was the way I put it. And after he had thoroughly examined my color, my wrinkles, my looks, he said that I was the likeliest to follow.

He had, however, asked me what I imagined death would be like – and when I said that the pictures would stop he reflected seriously on my answer, came to a full stop, and considered what I might mean by this. No one can give up on the pictures - the pictures might, yes they might continue. I wonder if anyone believes that the grave is all there is. No one can give up on pictures. The pictures must and will continue. If Ravelstein the atheist-materialist had implicitly told me that he would see me sooner or later, he meant that he did not accept the grave to be the end. Nobody can and nobody does accept this. We just talk tough.

Saul Bellow, Ravelstein

Receiving

My sister and I always celebrate the anniversary of our mother's death on July 29. One day when my sister went to check the calendar in the kitchen and put a circle around the date, she said "Hi Mom!" and gave it a kiss.

A little while later, when she went back to the kitchen, she noticed the microwave oven was on. She was sure she had not turned it on herself. When she looked further, it read "hi."

We both believe this was mom responding to us and sending us a message back.

Mary Ann Dickson, A family story

Consolation

THE AFTERLIFE. Would it not be consoling and satisfying if all those who devoted their lives to the development of their natural talents, for the benefit of all, found bliss after their deaths, in a life of satisfaction in accordance with their dreams. While those who lived strictly as egotists....

Henri Matisse, Jazz

We all fear death and question our place in the universe. The artist's job is not to succumb to despair but to find the great antidote to the emptiness of existence.

Gertrude Stein, movie script, Midnight in Paris

Unending

I will remain by this river, thought Siddhartha…

He looked lovingly into the flowing water, into the transparent green, into the crystal lines of its wonderful design. He saw bright pearls rise from the depths, bubbles swimming on the mirror, sky blue reflected in them. The river looked at him with a thousand eyes – green, white, crystal, sky blue. How he loved this river, how it enchanted him, how grateful he was to it! In his heart he heard the newly awakened voice speak, and it said to him: "Love this river, stay by it, learn from it." Yes, he wanted to learn from it, he wanted to listen to it. It seemed to him that whoever understood this river and its secrets, would understand much more, many secrets, all secrets….

He saw the water continually flowed and flowed and yet it was always there; it was always the same and yet every moment it was new. Who could understand, conceive this? He did not understand it: he was only aware of a dim suspicion, a faint memory, divine voices.

Herman Hesse, Siddhartha

Journeying

"I am going, O Nokomis,
On a long and distant journey,
To the portals of the Sunset,
To the regions of the home-wind
To the Northwest wind, Keewaydin..
On the shore stood Hiawatha,
Turned and waved his hand at parting;
On the clear and luminous water
Launched his birch canoe for sailing,
From the pebbles of the margin
Shoved it forth into the water;
Whispered to it, "Westward! Westward!"
And with speed it darted forward.
And the evening sun descending
Set the clouds on fire with redness,
Burned the broad sky, like a prairie,
Left upon the level water
One long track and trail of splendor
Down whose stream, as down the river,
Westward Hiawatha
Sailed into the fiery sunset,
Sailed into the purple vapors,
Sailed into the dusk of evening.
And the people from the margin
Watched him floating, rising, sinking,
Till the birch canoe seemed lifted

High into that sea of splendor,
Till it sank into the vapors
Like the new moon slowly, slowly
Sinking in the purple distance.
And they said: "Farewell for ever!
Said, "Farewell, O Hiawatha!"
And the forests, dark and lonely
Moved through all their depths of darkness
Sighed: "Farewell, O Hiawatha!"
And the waves upon the margin
Rising, rippling on the pebbles,
Sobbed: "Farewell, O Hiawatha!"
And the heron, the Su-shu-gah,
From her haunts among the fen-lands,
Screamed: "Farewell, O Hiawatha!"
Thus departed Hiawatha,
Hiawatha the Beloved,
In the glory of the sunset,
In the purple mists of evening,
To the regions of the home-wing,
Of the Northwest wind Keewaydinn,
To the Islands of the Blessed,
To the kingdom of Ponemah,
To the land of the Hereafter!

Henry Wadsworth Longfellow, The Song of Hiawatha

Ongoing

"The river is everywhere at the same time, at the source and at the mouth, at the waterfall, at the ferry, at the current, in the ocean and in the mountains, everywhere, and that the present only exists for it, not the shadow of the past, nor the shadow of the future…

And when I learned that I reviewed my life and it was also a river, and Siddhartha the boy, Siddhartha the mature man, and Siddhartha the old man, were only separated by shadows, not through reality. Siddhartha's previous lives were also not in the past, and his death and his return to Brahma are not in the future. Nothing was, nothing will be, everything has reality and presence.

Herman Hesse, Siddhartha

Afterwords

"Everything will be alright in the end. So if it's not alright, then it is not yet the end."
The Best Exotic Marigold Hotel movie

"When you are overwhelmed by disaster, just ponder this: May it not be that calamity has overtaken me in order for me to be forced to find the path of progress?"
Jain Master Chitrabhanu Speaks to One World.

"I am not afraid of death. I just don't want to be there when it happens."
Woody Allen

"Think of the end of your life not as checking out but as checking in to a new experience."
Mary McGeachy

Dh. Kiranada

Dh. Kiranada (Kiranada Sterling Benjamin), visual artist, author, and teacher has been practicing Buddhism since 1985, while living in Japan for 18 years. She was ordained in the Triratna Buddhist Order in 2009, guides the Contemplative Arts Program at Aryaloka Buddhist Center (Newmarket NH) and teaches at Massachusetts College of Art, Boston.

Beverly Russell

An internationally published writer and journalist, Beverly Russell was born in London in 1934. She has written over a dozen books on the arts and spiritual themes. The titles are available on Amazon.com. In 1967 she emigrated to the United States to pursue a career in publishing in New York City. In 1972 she became an American citizen. She has received many awards for her work, including two Honorary Doctorates in Fine Arts and a Citation from the American Academy in Rome. August 26 1986 was named "Beverly Russell Day" in New York City by Mayor Edward Koch. www.beverlyrussell.com

Barry Michlin

Born in the United States, Barry Michlin has been a photographer for over 50 years. An international traveler in France, Italy, England, Germany, Norway and Mexico, he is known for his exceptionally perceptive camera work and for capturing mystical sensations of light. He has had exhibitions of his photographs in numerous galleries, including New York City, Rome, Paris and Los Angeles, where his work has been exhibited at the Los Angeles County Museum of Art. His photographs have also been published in numerous books and magazines. He currently resides in Los Angeles, California. www.barrymichlin.com

List of Photographs by Barry Michlin

Cover Page	"Cereus"
8	"Givre-Giverville"
10	"Tevere Fantasia"
12	"Angelo Tramonto"
14	"Harp"
17	"Chambord Lumiere"
19	"Fellini-Tree"
21	"Bay of Salerno"
23	"Bella Addormentata"
25	"Le Poulain"
27	"A Heaven"
29	"Chartres Stained"
31	"Moutons-Normandie"
33	"La Tristesse-Pere Lachaise"
35	"Before the Ice Melts"
37	"Farfala-Mugnano"
39	"Chartres-Les Bougies"
41	"Tears of the Flower"
43	"From Tamalpais"
45	"Le Givre et Les Pommes"
47	"Wings of Crane"
49	"Chartres Gloria"
51	"Fishkill l"
53	"Star Sun"
55	"Louvre Pyramide"
57	"La Mare Versailles"
59	"Ponte Milvio-Tramonto"
61	"Roma Cielo"
63	"Brunno's Circle"
64	"Fishkill ll"
68	"Venice-A Golden Mean"
70	"New Paltz"

Individual prints of all these photographs are available.

Further information www.michlin light.com or email barrymichlin@hotmail.com

Index to Quotations

Dr. Lauren Artress, launched a rediscovery of the classical labyrinth from Chartres, France, when she was Canon for Special Ministries at Grace Cathedral, San Francisco. She is creator and founder of Veriditas, the Labyrinth Project, lectures and leads labyrinth workshops all over the world. "Walking the Sacred Path," was published in 1995.

Saul Bellow, 1915-2005, was a Canadian-born American writer. For his literary contributions he was awarded the Pulitzer Prize, the Nobel Prize in Literature and the National Medal of Arts. He is the only writer to win the National book Award for Fiction 3 times. "Ravelstein" was published in 2000.

Joseph Campbell, 1859-1944 was an Irish poet and lyricist, founder of the Ulster Literary Theatre in 1904. He emigrated to the USA in 1925 and lectured at Fordham University, before returning to Ireland in 1939.

Agatha Christie, DBE 1880-1976, was a British crime writer of novels, short stories and plays, the most famous featuring Hercule Poirot and Miss Marple. According to the Guiness Book of Record, she is the best-selling novelist of all time. "Passengers to Frankfurt" was published in 1979.

The 14th Dalai Lama is thought to be the latest reincarnation of a long line of spiritual leaders of the Yellow Hat branch of Tibetan Buddhism. He has lived in exile in India since 1959. The Dalai Lama's "Book of Wisdom" was published in 1995.

Mary Ann Dickson is a critical observer of political and social events. Born a New Yorker, she has traveled extensively and now lives in the South.

Thomas Stearns Eliot, 1988-1965, (T.S. Eliot) was a publisher, playwright and literary and social critic. American born, he became a British subject in 1927. He was awarded the Nobel Prize in Literature in 1948. Originally written as a verse drama, "Sweeney Agonistes," was incomplete, and eventually published as "Fragments of an Aristophanic Melodrama" in 1932.

Katharine Graham, 1912-2004, was CEO of the Washington Post, piloting the paper through the Pentagon Papers and Watergate crises. Her best selling life story "Personal History" was published in 1998 and won a Pulitzer Prize.

Robert Herrick, 1591-1674, was an English poet who wrote over 2500 poems. The over-riding message in his mostly pastoral works is that life is short, the world is beautiful, love is splendid and we must make the most of it in the short time we have. "To Virgins to Make Most of Time," is one of his most popular poems.

Herman Hesse, 1877-1962, was a German-Swiss poet, novelist and painter. He received the Nobel Prize in Literature in 1946. "Siddharta," published in 1922 is one of the most popular Western novels set in India and received a revival in 1960's. His major work "Magister Ludi" (The Glass Bead Game) was published in 1943.

Carl Gustav Jung, 1875-1961, a Swiss psychologist and psychiatrist, founded analytical psychology. His works has been influential in religion, literature, dream analysis and related medical fields. The popular Myers Briggs Type Indicator was developed from Jung's theories. His collected writings fill 19 volumes.

Lao Tzu, was keeper of the Chinese Imperial archives in the sixth century BC. According to legend, as he was riding off into the desert to die, he was persuaded to write down his teaching, Tao Te Ching. These 5000 words have since provided the underlying influence of Chinese thought and culture for 2500 years.

Geri Larkin, a one-time successful American management consultant became a practicing Buddhist in 1988 and was ordained in 1995. She is a Zen Buddhist dharma teacher and author of several spiritual books. "Plant Seed, Pull Weed," was published in 2008.

Henry Wadsworth Longfellow, 1807-1882, was an American poet, novelist and educator, professor at Bowdoin College and Harvard University. He retired from teaching in 1854 to concentrate on writing. "The Song of Hiawatha," one of his most popular lyric poems was written in 1855.

Henri Matisse, 1869-1954, was a French artist, printmaker and sculptor, regarded as one of the major artists of the early 20th century. Many of his paintings are in major museums all over the world. "Jazz," his book of over 100 prints based on paper cutouts was published in 1947.

Thomas Merton, 1915-1968, was an Anglo-American Trappist monk, writer and mystic. Author of more than 70 books, he pioneered a dialog with prominent Asian spiritual leaders. "Wisdom of the Desert, Sayings from the Desert Fathers of the Fourth Century," was translated and published in 1960.

Christina Georgina Rosetti, 1830-1894, an English poet in the reign of Queen Victoria, published her first works at 18. By the time she was 30, she was considered the leading female poet of her era. She is best known for the verses to the Christmas carol "In the Bleak Mid-Winter."

Dr. Robert Sapolsky, Professor of Neurology and Neurosurgery at Stanford University, is the recipient of a MacArthur "genius" grant. "A Guide to Stress, Stress-Related Diseases, and Coping" published in 2004, was a finalist in the Los Angeles Times Book Award. The work is the subject of 24 lectures comprising one of The Great Courses.

Gertrude Stein, 1874-1946 was an American writer, poet and art collector who spent most of her life in France. Much of her fame derives from a private modern art collection of works by Cezanne, Renoir, Picasso, Gaugin, Matisse and other impressionists, now in the Baltimore Museum of Art.

Rabindranath Tagore, 1861-1941, was a Bengali polymath who wrote his first poetry at age 8 and his first substantial collection of poems at 16. He is generally regarded as one of the most creative artists of modern India. He became the first non-European to win the Nobel Prize in Literature in 1913.

Alfred Tennyson, 1st Baron Tennyson, 1809-1902, was Poet Laureate of the United Kingdom during Queen Victoria's reign. Tennyson excelled at short lyrics such as "The Charge of the Light Brigade." "Idylls of the King," written in blank verse, was first published in 1900.

J.R.R Tolkien (John Ronald Reuel), 1892-1973, was an English writer, poet, philologist and university professor best known as the author of classic high fantasy works. "The Road Goes On and On," is one of the walking songs in "The Hobbit," written about 1925.

CPSIA information can be obtained
at www.ICGtesting.com
Printed in the USA
LVIC06n2114291013
359126LV00012B/161

9 780976 290537